GOD Is Love

Guidelines to Biblical Intercessory Prayer

"You are All That I Need"; Coll. 3:11

Dear Bruce. Thank you so much for your special part in the process of the booklet. May our LORD bless you and your family continually!

Anita Sebastian

Anita Sebastian

Nov. 1, 2021

TEACH Services, Inc.
P U B L I S H I N G
www.TEACHServices.com • (800) 367-1844

Copyright © 2021 Anita Sebastian
Copyright © 2021 TEACH Services, Inc.
ISBN-13: 978-1-4796-1449-3 (Paperback)
ISBN-13: 978-1-4796-1377-9 (ePub)
ISBN-13: 978-1-4796-1376-2 (Saddle Stitch)
Library of Congress Control Number: 2021914506

Published by

TEACH Services, Inc.
PUBLISHING
www.TEACHServices.com • (800) 367-1844

About the Cover

A dove among clouds was selected as a symbol of peace and to represent the Holy Spirit—the third person of the Trinity who guides our prayers. The olive branch in the dove's beak reminds us of the abated waters after the worldwide Flood. The clouds represent where the GOD of Love resides, and where He longs for us to reside. Knowing that our Savior will soon return with clouds to take us to Heaven is the Promised Hope of all believers. But time is running out for *others*. Needed are intercessory prayers on behalf of lost souls ... before it's too late.

Acknowledgements

"Not unto us, O LORD, not unto us, but to Your name give glory, because of Your mercy, because of Your truth" (Psalm 115:1).

I'm so grateful to my heavenly Father for His mercy and grace in my life and for giving me this precious prayer to share with my brethren.

Thank you to my dear husband, Josef, for his support and faithfulness and for his Christlike patience and faithful prayers while I worked on completing this project.

I would like to express my heartfelt appreciation for my spiritual friends: Patricia H., Glen S., Carole and Bill M. (Canadians), and Bruce D. (American) for their support and help in this project. Several pastors have been a great support: Pastor S. Mawutor, Pastor E. Emerson, Pastor S. MacFarlane (all Canadians), and Pastor A. Kessie from Ghana. A special appreciation to my original editor, CJ (American), who spent many hours with me, formatting, editing, and polishing these guidelines in the early stages of this booklet. Each helper, however, will agree: *All the glory goes to GOD.*

Anita Sebastian

Table of Contents

Introduction

What is Intercessory Prayer?

Intercessory prayer is unselfish, biblical prayer on behalf of others.

The prayer format in this booklet was originally written for a young Latvian lady who wanted to better understand the depths of intercessory prayer. It started out as seven pages; but then something unexpected happened. GOD broadened the vision—that the prayer could be used by many. Over more than a year, I felt led to add more material and polish it. It grew to ten pages.

I know I was blessed by my Heavenly Father, but there still wasn't peace. With every day and month my understanding grew, yet I kept searching to know my Father's will. Step-by-step He opened my understanding and encouraged me with new ideas. But I was so disappointed that after all the work and all the prayer, I could not share the booklet—even with my Canadian husband because he could not read Latvian! It needed to also be in English.

GOD led me to someone who became a close, spiritual friend, a pastor's wife from Albania—Sanda Veidemane Thomollari—who helped translate it. GOD gave me another friend and spiritual sister, "CJ," from the United States, a proofreader and professional editor who formatted it into a professional-looking book. The hours which we worked on this project are now uncountable.

It was hard work because just when I thought the booklet was done, I felt another wave of improvements would make it wider, deeper, richer. From ten pages it grew to thirty. I didn't understand then, but now I realize that our prayers will never be complete. Each moment, we can come to a deeper understanding of GOD's love, mercies, and will. He will give us a fresh view and understanding every day.

I believe that's how our prayers and our relationship with our Father in Heaven should be: not rushed or stressed, but taking the necessary time, constantly growing in Christ, developing and maturing, reaching deeper and expanding wider. Our daily prayers should not be repetitive, monotonous, or without thinking; but fresh, as opening our heart and talking with our best friend.

Christ's disciples asked, "Lord, teach us how to pray." Let us each ask the same. To contemplate in prayer is not the same as the New Age contemplative prayer being erroneously taught in some churches and theological seminaries. Prayer should never resemble mindless, Eastern (transcendental) meditation, allowing evil influences into our minds, but rather we should meditate by thinking deeply about GOD's Holy Word and the life of Christ.

It is important to claim GOD's promises as we pray. The Bible contains about 8,800 promises, most of which we are privileged to claim as our own. This booklet contains only about 160, so feel free to add your own as you study. Claiming these promises every time we pray helps commit them to memory; and memorizing scripture helps our faith grow and places us in a position to receive the divine power that is behind each promise.

The sample prayer helps build our trust, but it will take time just as a closer relationship takes time. And that is exactly what our loving Father wants from us—a closer relationship. So, we must find time to spend with Him. We must spend time and energy praying, treating it as a serious job, because prayer is where we fight spiritual battles over the souls of those who need intercession as well as our own!

As you better understand the main points of this prayer, personalize it as a prayer from your own heart. Create a list of the names of people you know—relatives, friends, neighbors, and acquaintances from all stages of life and in various settings, from childhood, adulthood, home, school, work, etc. Pray for the Holy Spirit to remind you of every name. Select a name from among the people you pray for and insert it as you pray. I like to add: "and his family" or "and her children" if I don't know their names. In places coming later in the prayer, you could simply say "all the mentioned people." This is how I do my daily praying for as many people on my list as possible. I also present before GOD the list as a whole.

At the end of his life, Roger Morneau, the well-known prayer warrior, had a 150-page notebook containing 27,000 names, and he called aloud hundreds of those names daily. My experience is far less, but my list has grown from a few hundred to well over 3,000. I have seen the great benefits of this model of prayer. I have seen how our enemy, Satan, hates this kind of prayer and how he tries to make me tired, busy, etc. to stop me from praying it. When I see his attack, I know I am on the right track.

Please pray for the people in this dying, sinful world. Everybody needs prayer. People need to know that you are praying for them, even if they do not believe or understand the power of prayer. Remember that GOD has placed them on *your* heart, so answer His call to pray for them whether or not they are believers. Only in prayer and trusting GOD's promises can we be strong in Him and win precious souls for eternity.

Praise and Thanksgiving

Praise and thanksgiving don't come naturally for many, but I learned it is a very important introduction to our prayers and should be more than a few sentences long. I had to learn how by training my heart to stay in this state. It was through praise and thanksgiving that I found my own spirit and faith strengthened.

Practice this in your own prayers! Make some of your prayers *only* those of thanksgiving, without asking for a thing. You will find that the more you practice and ask GOD to remind you of past and present blessings, the easier it becomes to maintain a grateful attitude in prayer and in your day-to-day life. What a confidence builder!

We need to constantly remind ourselves that GOD is the Creator of all things, holy, powerful, First and Last, the Bread of Life, my Helper, the Prince of Peace, a Mighty Rock, our Savior, Redeemer, the Alpha and the Omega, All in All, my best Friend, and loving Father. What can we ask or tell our Father what He doesn't already know? And, if He knows all our lives and needs before we even ask, let's spend more time praising Him and giving thanks for His individual plans for each person because of His unimaginable love.

Suggestions on How to Best Use This Book

We must be much more with God in earnest prayer. We must make God our only trust.

This is not a book to read and put back on the shelf. I use my copy as a workbook, constantly adding names, jotting down ideas, and adding promises that I come across in my Bible study time.

While the prayer in this booklet is one complete prayer, each section can be prayed separately. When you start using this outline, you can just read the suggested wording until you become more familiar with the format. As you do this, our Father will lead you to better understand what to pray for, who to pray for, and how to pray.

One page has been left largely blank to begin your own prayer list. That space will likely fill up quickly. I use sticky notes to write down people's names and stick them in the book in the sections that are especially needed in their lives. Where you see blank spaces, _____, you are invited to say the names on your list aloud.

Asking for the Baptism of the Holy Spirit

"Bless the LORD, O my soul; and all that is within me, bless His holy name! Bless the LORD, O my soul, and forget not all His benefits[!]" (Psalm 103:1, 2).

The Baptism of the Holy Spirit: It is important to daily ask for a fresh baptism of the Holy Spirit. He is as much a person as are the Father and Son. The Holy Spirit, Himself God, knows the Father and reveals the Father to us in a trustworthy manner. Sent by the Father and Son to be always with His children, the Holy Spirit points to Jesus and the marvelous things He has done for us.

O LORD my GOD, this moment my heart is filled with gratitude and praises, this is my dearest moment to sit at Your feet, spend time with You, study Your Word, and pray: Father, teach me what and how to pray. Refresh me and baptize with Your Holy Spirit by Your promises:

Luke 11:13 "How much more will *your* heavenly Father give the Holy Spirit to those who ask Him."

Galatians 3:14 "That we might receive the promise of the Spirit through faith."

Ephesians 1:13 "You were sealed with the Holy Spirit of promise."

Acts 1:5 "For John truly baptized with water, but you shall be baptized with the Holy Spirit."

The Holy Spirit, GOD Himself, knows GOD and reveals GOD to us in a trustworthy manner.

John 15:26 "But when the Helper comes, whom I shall send to you from the Father, the Spirit of truth who proceeds from the Father, He will testify of Me."

John 4:24 "God *is* Spirit, and those who worship Him must worship in spirit and truth."

1 Peter 4:14 "The Spirit of glory and of God rests upon you."

1 Corinthians 3:16 "Do you know that you are the temple of God and that the Spirit of God dwells in you?"

"But you are not in the flesh but in the Spirit, if indeed the Spirit of God dwells in you" (Romans 8:9).

Praying Step 2

Give Unto GOD Glory and Thanks

"Let them praise the name of the LORD, for His name alone is exalted; His glory *is* above the earth and heaven" (Psalm 148:13).

Psalm 89:11 "The heavens *are* Yours, the earth also *is* Yours; the world and all its fullness, You have founded them."

Psalm 93:1, 2 "The LORD reigns, He is clothed with majesty…Surely the world is established, so that it cannot be moved. Your throne *is* established from of old; You *are* from everlasting."

Psalm 96:6 "Honor and majesty *are* before Him; strength and beauty *are* in His sanctuary."

Psalm 11:4 "The LORD *is* in His holy temple, the LORD's throne *is* in heaven; His eyes behold, His eyelids test the sons of men."

Psalm 33:6 "By the word of the LORD the heavens were made, and all the host of them by the breath of His mouth."

Psalm 100:3 "*We are* His people and the sheep of His pasture."

Psalm 96:13 "For He is coming to judge the earth. He shall judge the world with righteousness, and the people with His truth."

Psalm 89:14 "Righteousness and justice *are* the foundation of Your throne; Mercy and truth go before Your face."

Isaiah 33:22 "For the LORD *is* our Judge, the LORD *is* our Lawgiver, the LORD *is* our King; He will save us."[1]

Isaiah 40:28 "The everlasting God, the LORD, the Creator of the ends of the earth…His understanding is unsearchable."

Habakkuk 3:4 "*His* brightness was like the light; He had rays *flashing* from His hand, and there His power *was* hidden."

Psalm 147:4, 5 "He counts the number of the stars; He calls them all by name. Great *is* our Lord, and mighty in power; His understanding *is* infinite."

Revelation 4:11 "You are worthy, O Lord, to receive glory and honor and power; for You created all things, and by Your will they exist and were created."

Revelation 19:1 "Alleluia! Salvation and glory and honor and power *belong* to the Lord our God!"

"Let heaven and earth praise Him" (Psalm 69:34).

---

[1]See "Law/Commandments" in the Topical Bible Reference Index.

Almighty GOD, hallowed is Your Name. Blessed are You who live in unimaginable majesty, holiness, glory, and power. All heaven cannot fully comprehend You. How can our finite minds grasp who You are, Your greatness and might? I can only say, "Thank you, my dear Father, holy GOD, that I can be Your dear child. I know You love me with Your unconditional, everlasting love. Amen and Amen."

The Lord God, *Merciful and Gracious*

"And the Lord…proclaimed, 'The Lord, the Lord God, merciful and gracious, longsuffering, and abounding in goodness
and truth, keeping mercy for thousands, forgiving iniquity and
transgression and sin'" (Exodus 34:6, 7).

Isaiah 63:16 "You, O Lord, *are* our Father; Our Redeemer from
Everlasting *is* Your name."

Jeremiah 31:3 "I have loved you with an everlasting love; therefore with
lovingkindness I have drawn you."

Romans 5:5 "The love of God has been poured out in our hearts by the
Holy Spirit who was given to us."

Psalm 8:4–6 "What is man that You are mindful of him, and the son of
man that You visit him? For You have made him a little lower than
the angels, and You have crowned him with glory and honor. You
have made him to have dominion over the work of Your hands; You
have put all *things* under his feet."

God is love. His mercy endures forever.

Our loving Father, Your Word claims that You are Love—an eternal love![2]
*We can see Your love in Your creation. How marvelously everything is
done. If Your love is so beautifully represented in tiny snowflakes, how
much more is it reflected in mankind—the crowning work of Creation.
You made man in Your image, a little lower than the angels. You offer Your
love that is everlasting—a love that never ends.*

---

[2]See 1 John 4:7, 8, 16.

Psalm 103:17 "But the mercy of the LORD *is* from everlasting to everlasting on those who fear Him."

Romans 8:38, 39 "Neither death nor life, nor angels nor principalities nor powers, nor things present nor things to come, nor height nor depth, nor any other created thing, shall be able to separate us from the love of God which is in Christ Jesus our Lord."

Romans 8:32 "He who did not spare His own Son, but delivered Him up for us all, how shall He not with Him also freely give us all things?"

Galatians 3:26 "For you are all sons of God through faith in Christ Jesus."

Christ died for us so that we could live in You, Merciful Father. Your love is truly deep! We cannot even begin to grasp it. Thank You for loving us so much.

Psalm 68:19 "Blessed *be* the Lord, *Who* daily loads us *with benefits*, the God of our salvation!"

Take time counting your blessings and thanking Him for each one, big or seemingly small, that comes to mind, such as: protection, food, clothing, shelter, loved ones, life, etc.

"For God so loved the world that He gave His only begotten Son, that whoever believes in Him should not perish but have everlasting life" (John 3:16).

Thank You, Father!

Praying Step 4

Contemplation of the Cross

"For the Son of Man has come to seek and to save that which was lost" (Luke 19:10).

Before you contemplate the cross, please read Matthew 27 with a focus on the story of Calvary in verses 27–55. You can also read it in the three other gospels: Mark 15, Luke 23, and John 18:28–19:30.

It is an important suggestion to *read and contemplate the cross of Jesus Christ every day*. It changes our hearts and lives in miraculous ways. If it weren't for His sacrificial death on the cross, we would die in our sins.[3]

Hebrews 1:3 "[Christ,] who being the brightness of *His* [**God's**] glory and the express image of His [**God's**] person...when He had by

---

[3]See "Sin" and "Death and Resurrection" in the Topical Bible Reference Index.

Himself purged our sins,[4] sat down at the right hand of the Majesty on high."

Luke 19:10 "For the Son of Man has come to seek and to save that which was lost."

2 Corinthians 5:21 "For He made Him who knew no sin to *be* sin for us, that we might become the righteousness of God in Him."

Romans 6:23 "For the wages of sin *is* death,[5] but the gift of God is eternal life in Christ Jesus our Lord."

2 Corinthians 5:19 "That God was in Christ reconciling the world to Himself."

Colossians 1:20 "By Him, whether things on earth or things in heaven, having made peace through the blood of His cross."

Dear Savior, You laid down Your life, because of our sins. You are the Lamb of GOD who takes away the sin of the world,[6] therefore GOD has given us eternal life, and this life is in His Son.[7] LORD Jesus Christ, You are a perfect bridge between the holy, eternal GOD and sinful finite humanity. "You are the way, the truth, and the life."[8]

Ephesians 2:4–7 "But God who is rich in mercy, because of His great love with which He loved us, even when we were dead in trespasses, made us alive together with Christ (by grace you have been saved), and raised *us* up together, and made *us* sit together in the heavenly *places* in Christ Jesus, that in the ages to come He might

---

[4]See "Sin" in the Topical Bible Reference Index.
[5]See "Sin" in the Topical Bible Reference Index.
[6]See John 1:29.
[7]See 1 John 5:11.
[8]See John 14:6.

show the exceeding riches of His grace in *His* kindness toward us in Christ Jesus."

In Your love for us, and with Your Holy Spirit, You are trying to reach each one's heart.

We belong to Jesus Christ and together with You, there is no condemnation. In Your love for us, and with Your Holy Spirit, You are trying to reach each one's heart.

"Behold, I stand at the door and knock. If anyone hears My voice and opens the door, I will come in to him and dine with him, and he with Me. To him who overcomes I will grant to sit with Me on My throne" (Revelation 3:20, 21).

Thank You for Your promise.

Create in Me a Clean Heart

"Create in me a clean heart, O God, And renew a steadfast spirit within me. Do not cast me away from Your presence, And do not take Your Holy Spirit from me" (Psalm 51:10, 11).

I confess my sins.

Psalm 71:8 "Let my mouth be filled *with* Your praise *And with* Your glory all the day!"

Your mercy is great toward me.

Romans 3:23 "For all have sinned and fall short of the glory of God."

Because of our sinful human nature and bad characters, we are prone to failing. Many times, we need to admit that:

Romans 7:15 "For what I am doing, I do not understand. For what I will to do, that I do not practice; but what I hate, that I do."

We are selfish and self-righteous. And Your enemy tries to attack our minds, invading our thoughts seemingly constantly.[9] Please keep evil away with Your cleansing blood.

Read Psalm 51 and use verses as a prayer. For example, you may pray:

"Have mercy on me, O GOD, according to Your lovingkindness; according to the multitude of Your tender mercies, blot out my transgressions."[10]

---

[9]See "Satan/Devil" in the Topical Bible Reference Index.
[10]Psalm 51:1.

"Create in me a clean heart, O God, and renew a steadfast spirit within me."[11] "Restore to me the joy of Your salvation and uphold me by Your generous Spirit."[12]

Take your time. Confess your sins. But which ones? Confess each one that God reveals to you. It is not enough to say: Please forgive all my sins! We have to recognize our sins.

Abba Father, please show me if there is anything that has hurt You recently. Maybe my words or actions have hurt somebody without my knowing? Please show me every situation.

Also pray for God to reveal every sin that:

- may be *unknown* to you.
- you are *harboring*, keeping in your heart some negative attitudes toward others. *That is sin.*
- reveals *unforgiveness* in you. Ask for victory to forgive that person. It is an important part.

1 John 1:9 "If we confess our sins, He is faithful and just to forgive us *our* sins and to cleanse us from all unrighteousness."[13]

Ephesians 1:7 In Jesus Christ, "We have redemption through His blood, the forgiveness of sins, according to the riches of His grace."

"But you [the church at Corinth] were washed, but you were sanctified, but you were justified in the name of the Lord Jesus and by the Spirit of our God" (1 Corinthians 6:11).

---

[11]Psalm 51:10.
[12]Psalm 51:12.
[13]**Unrighteousness**: Unholiness, wrongdoing, everything that is not in conformity with God's Word, His will, and His purposes.

Merciful Father, if I confess, You will forgive my sin. I am cleansed, and my Savior covers me with the pure, white robe of His righteousness[14]. I now believe that I am justified[15] before You in Christ's righteousness, and that You will accept my prayers for others as well. Amen.

---

[14]**Righteousness**: Right doing. See Psalm 119:172.
[15]**Justified:** JUST-IF-IED (JUST-as-IF-I'D never sinned!) Justify: to regard or treat as righteous and worthy of salvation.

Praying Step 6

Presenting the List of Names

Loving Father, at this moment my heart is sad that there are so many around the world and around me who don't believe and don't want to hear Your message of love, grace, and truth.

1 Timothy 2:3, 4 "For this *is* good and acceptable in the sight of God our Savior, who desires **all men** to be saved and to come to the knowledge of the truth."

Ephesians 2:8 "For by grace you have been saved through faith, and that not of yourselves; *it is the gift of God.*"

Father, You encourage us to pray for those who still don't have trust, faith, and understanding of Your amazing gift in Christ Jesus. You encourage us not to give up, but to continue earnestly praying for them.

James 5:20 "He who turns a sinner from the error of his way will save a soul from death."

Ephesians 6:12, 13, 17, 18 "For we do not wrestle against flesh and blood, but against principalities, against powers, against the rulers of the darkness of this age, against spiritual *hosts* of wickedness in heavenly *places*. Therefore, take up the whole armor of God...the sword of the Spirit, which is the word of God; praying always with all prayer and supplication in the Spirit."

Acts 16:31 "Believe on the Lord Jesus Christ, and you will be saved, you and your household."

O LORD GOD, we have to use the whole armor against the rulers of darkness and the evil powers. Help us to trust in Your promises, knowing that You will answer the desires of our hearts, because of Your promises.

Present Your List of Names

Use the space below to begin your list of people to remember in prayer.

_____

_____

_____

_____

_____

_____

_____

_____

_____

Plea to Redeem All from Captivity by the Power of Christ's Blood

2 Timothy 1:7 "For God has not given us a spirit of fear, but of power and of love and of a sound mind."

James 4:7 "Therefore submit to God. Resist the devil[16] and he will flee from you."

Ephesians 6:10, 11 "Be strong in the Lord and in the power of His might. Put on the whole armor of God, that you may be able to stand against the wiles of the devil."

1 John 3:8 "For the devil has sinned from the beginning. For this purpose the Son of God was manifested, that He might destroy the works of the devil."

Almighty GOD, *I trust that only You can destroy the works of the devil, Your enemy, who is still alive and keeps his prisoners in darkness and bondage. I believe the power of Your promises and I claim them in the lives of _____. Please intervene, release, discharge, and redeem _____ from all addictions and slavery by Your promises.*

Psalm 146:7 "The LORD gives freedom to the prisoners." _____

Isaiah 49:25 "Even the captives of [Satan] _____ shall be taken away."

---

[16]See "Satan/Devil" in the Topical Bible Reference Index.

Knowing that _____ *are redeemed with the precious blood of Christ.*[17]

1 John 3:8 "The Son of God was manifested, that He might destroy the works of the devil" *in* _____*'s life.*

That through His death the LORD *might destroy him who had power over death, that is, the devil, and release* _____ *who through fear of death were all their lifetime subject to bondage.*[18]

Satan is defeated by the power of Christ's holy blood, and _____ *are delivered from the power of darkness.* _____ *are conveyed into Christ's kingdom.*

Loving Father, please speak to _____*'s mind, to understand and embrace this truth that You are the Savior who will help* _____ *to get freedom from all bondage and slavery. May the Holy Spirit overpower and nullify, in* _____*'s life, the power of sin, the power of death, and the power of separation from* GOD! *Amen.*

Father, please, send Your guardian angels to guard and protect _____. *May the power of Your glory be like a wall of fire, blocking all the evil that is trying to manipulate* _____*'s mind.*

In Your love You came to heal the brokenhearted

In Your love You came to heal the brokenhearted, to proclaim liberty to the captives, and recovery of sight to the blind, cause the deaf to hear and the mute to speak[19] *Please open* _____*'s spiritual mind, ears, and eyes to understand Your help and glorify You. Amen.*

---

[17]See 1 Peter 1:18, 19.
[18]See Hebrews 2:14, 15.
[19]See Luke 4:18 and Mark 9:17–27.

Praying Step 8

Prayer for Repentance, Cleansing, and a New Character

"To Him who loved us and washed us from our sins in His own blood...to Him be glory and dominion forever and ever. Amen" (Revelation 1:5, 6).

O Lord God, _____ still err in spirit, not understanding their situation, their sinful life, and their own bad choices, but Your promise gives us hope that those "who erred in spirit will come to understanding."[20]

---

[20]Isaiah 29:24.

Christ Jesus, You prayed on the cross, "Father, forgive them, for they do not know what they do."[21] *That is why I am praying for _____ also, Father, forgive _____, for they do not know what they are doing!*

*Let Your light shine upon _____ to see the truth of this world's sinfulness. Please, help _____ to look at his/her sinful life; to analyze it and to understand how desperately he/she needs You as Savior. Please, give _____ the **will** to ask for Your help to hate the sin and **wish** for changes.*

Loving Father, You promised, "I am He who blots out transgressions for My own sake; and I will not remember your sins."[22] *Amen.*

2 Timothy 2:25 "God perhaps will grant them repentance, so that they may know the truth."

Please grant _____ the help to repent and ask for forgiveness.

Isaiah 65:1, 2 "I was sought by *those* who did not ask *for Me*; I was found by *those who* did not seek Me. I said, 'Here I am, here I am,' To a nation *that* was not called by My name. I have stretched out My hands all day long to a rebellious people, Who walk in a way *that is* not good, according to their own thoughts."

Dear Father, please lead _____ to a deeper understanding of Your loving, merciful character, and of how much You love them.

Please purify and transform _____'s character into Your image; with a quiet spirit, and a humble, soft, loving heart who will trust, obey, and love You as his/her Savior and loving Father. Please help _____ day by day to grow in Your wisdom and love. Father, please soften _____'s heart.

---

[21] Luke 23:34.
[22] Isaiah 43:25.

Hebrews 4:7 "**Today**, if you will hear His voice, do not harden your hearts."

*Please, help it be **today**, that _____ can hear Your call, the voice of the Holy Spirit, opening his/her heart, allowing You to come in and letting You lead his/her life. L*ORD* Jesus, I am claiming Your promises:*

John 10:9 "**I am the door**. If anyone enters by Me, he will be saved, and will go in and out and find pasture."

"I am the good Shepherd…My sheep hear My voice, and I know them, and they follow Me. And I give them eternal life, and they shall never perish; neither shall anyone snatch them out of My hand" (John 10:11, 27, 28).

*O L*ORD*, I know that with the power of Your Holy Spirit, You will do everything to bring _____ into Your flock; to be Your sheep who hears Your voice and follows You wherever You will lead and no one will snatch _____ out of Your hand. Amen.*

Today Is Your Salvation and Re-Creation

"In an acceptable time I have heard you, and in the day of salvation I have helped you" (2 Corinthians 6:2).

"For this is the covenant that I will make with [them]…says the Lord: I will put My laws[23] in _____'s mind(s) and write them on _____'s heart(s); and I will be their God, and _____ shall be My people."

LORD, *You want to give _____ a new, loving, obedient heart and a new Spirit.*

Precious Father, please recreate _____ mentally, emotionally, and spiritually into a new creation; someone who wants to "seek those things which are above."[24] Please give _____ a thirst for You, to open and study Your word, growing deeper with understanding of Your divine character. Teach _____ to talk with You, to ask Your advice in every situation. LORD *please open _____'s spiritual understanding, to see and appreciate Your help, to experience success and the benefits of Your guidance.*

2 Corinthians 5:17 "Therefore, if anyone *is* in Christ, *he is* a new creation; old things have passed away; behold, all things have become new."

Thank you, Father, for removing _____'s friends who are not from You. Please send Your children across _____'s path to become faithful friends who would love, help, and encourage them. Please, help _____ to find comfort, peace, and joy in the new lifestyle which will

---

[23]See "Law" in the Topical Bible Reference Index.
[24]Colossians 3:1.

give _____ unlimited opportunities to use Your given talents and new spiritual gifts for Your honor and glory. Father in heaven, please guard with Your angels each person, because the enemy will try to lure them back.

Please teach _____ to discern between Your silent voice, the voice of the Holy Spirit, and the voice of the enemy (Satan). Strengthen _____ to stand in Your power against all deceptions and temptations, claiming Your promise: "For in that He Himself has suffered, being tempted, He is able to aid those who are tempted."[25]

Please bind _____ to You with strong, unbreakable ropes so that no storm, nor powers of darkness, can sever the connection with You, because "the eternal GOD is _____'s refuge, and underneath are the everlasting arms."[26]

NOTE: Please **take time and pray** for individuals who need jobs, healing, or divine help, etc., and present them to God.

I pray for Your Spirit to surround _____ with an atmosphere of peace and light, that _____ may place all their burdens at Your feet knowing how much You love them.

> **"Casting all your care upon Him, for He cares for you" (1 Peter 5:7).**

Thank You, my loving Father, for responding with Your love. Your plan for each one is perfect, for You make no mistakes.

---

[25]Hebrews 2:18.
[26]Deuteronomy 33:27.

Praying Step 10

Petition for Christ's Intercession

Christ Jesus, You are alive! You rose from the dead and ascended to heaven to continue Your mission of being GOD's Word, GOD's Son, GOD's Lamb in the Most Holy Place—in the heavenly Sanctuary.[27]

Hebrews 8:1, 2 "We have such a High Priest,[28] who is seated at the right hand of the throne of the Majesty in the heavens, a Minister of the sanctuary."

1 Timothy 2:5 "For *there* is one God and one Mediator between God and men, *the* Man Christ Jesus."

---

[27]See "Sanctuary" in the Topical Bible Reference Index.
[28]See "High Priest" in the Topical Bible Reference Index.

Hebrews 7:24, 25 "But He, because He continues forever, has an unchangeable priesthood. Therefore He is also able to save to the uttermost those who come to God through Him, since *He always lives to make intercession for them.*"

"...I...will draw all peoples to Myself."[29] All![30]

Lord Jesus, thank You for continuing Your intercessory ministry as our High Priest, petitioning to the Father for fallen humanity. Please engrave these names in Your breastplate: _____. May these precious souls always be close to Your heart, and be presented before the Father.[31]

NOTE: Each time you come to this section of your prayer, be sure to include any new names which you have added to your list for Christ's priestly ministry before the Father. This is His most important work and our most important need.

"In My Father's house are many mansions, if it were not so, I would have told you. I go to prepare a place for you. And if I go and prepare a place for you, I will come again and will receive you to Myself;[32] that where I am, there you may be also."[33] I believe _____ will be there.

Luke 10:20 "Rejoice because your names are written in heaven."

Philippians 3:20 "For our citizenship is in heaven, from which we also eagerly wait for the Savior, the Lord Jesus Christ."

My Savior, the name of each one of Your followers is written in heaven. Lord Jesus Christ, You promise to return and take us home. The most wonderful place is prepared for everyone who puts their trust in You.

---

[29]John 12:32.

[30]It is God's intention that everyone should be saved so you can claim this promise on behalf of everyone on your prayer list who does not have a relationship with Jesus.

[31]See Exodus 28:29.

[32]See "I will come again"/Christ's return" in the Topical Bible Reference Index.

[33]John 14:2, 3.

O Lord, I believe _____ *will be Your followers and will be part of that great multitude. We will be together, and with You, we will live forever in the New Jerusalem.*[34]

You [Jesus] said to Your Father: "Of those whom You gave me I have lost none."[35] *So, I place before You all on my list:* _____ *and believe that no one will be lost.*

Dear loving Father, also please help me not to give up, but to pray every day for these dear ones. Just as the Canaanite woman who begged You to save her daughter, I want to hear these words from You: "...great is your faith! Let it be to you as you desire."[36] *Amen.*

> **"...I looked, and behold, a great multitude which no one could number, of all nations, tribes, peoples, and tongues, standing before the throne and before the Lamb, clothed with white robes, with palm branches in their hands" (Revelation 7:9).**

---

[34]See "New Jerusalem" in the Topical Bible Reference Index.
[35]John 18:9.
[36]Matthew 15:28. Read full story in Matthew 15:21–28.

Seeking the Holy Spirit's Personal Guidance

Loving Abba (Daddy), here I am, Your dear child. You know the day, Your plan for my life, and how You would love to use me today. Please, lead me with Your Holy Spirit, open my understanding to Your guidance. I want to hear Your voice and suggestions in every situation. Please fill me with Your wisdom and protect me from all evil. Help me to be alert and not be deceived.

NOTE: Take your time, going through the day's schedule, praying for all situations.

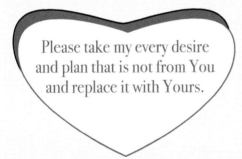

Please take my every desire and plan that is not from You and replace it with Yours.

Also, only You know what I really need—a humble, obedient heart "...to do justly, to love mercy, and to walk humbly with [my] God."[37] *Therefore, please take my every desire and plan that is not from You and replace it with Yours.*

Precious Father, our greatest need is love, and the ability to love unconditionally. Please break my selfishness and fill my heart with Your love and grace, that I—with Your compassionate, gentle touch—can reach dear souls around me. Give me boldness to be Your witness!

Acts 1:8 "But you shall receive power when the Holy Spirit has come upon you; and you shall be witnesses."

Please give me even one divine appointment to be Your witness, a blessing to even one person today. Grant me Your patience, Your peace, to

---

[37]Micah 6:8.

be blameless, with a heart thankful for everything, and always rejoicing in You.

Please, make me like Jesus. *May my personal life show to others that I am Your child.*

I am calling, like Jabez: *"Bless me indeed, and enlarge my territory, that Your hand would be with me, and that You would keep me from evil, that I may not cause pain!"*[38]

All Your guidelines, the blueprint for my life, are in Your Word, in Your promises. And I am putting total confidence and trust in them, because You, my loving Father, said:

Psalm 32:8 "I will instruct you and teach you in the way you should go."

Hebrews 13:5 "I will never leave you nor forsake you."

Matthew 28:20 "I am with you always, *even* to the end of the age."

Isaiah 41:10 "Fear not, for I *am* with you; be not dismayed, for I *am* your God. I will strengthen you, Yes, I will help you, I will uphold you with My righteous right hand."

Isaiah 40:29 "He gives power to the weak, and to *those who have* no might He increases strength."

Psalm 91:10, 11 "No evil shall befall you, nor shall any plague come near your dwelling; for He shall give His angels charge over you, To keep you in all your ways."

2 Timothy 1:7 "For God has not given us a spirit of fear, but of power and of love and of a sound mind."

---

[38] 1 Chronicles 4:10.

Proverbs 2:6 "For the LORD gives wisdom."

Rejoice in the LORD always!

Isaiah 26:3 "You will keep *him* in perfect peace, *Whose* mind is stayed *on You*, Because he trusts in You."

Psalm 91:7 "A thousand may fall at your side, And ten thousand at your right hand; But it [destruction] shall not come near you."

Deuteronomy 33:27 "The eternal God *is your* refuge, and underneath *are* the everlasting arms."

Philippians 4:13 "I can do all things through Christ who strengthens me."

Philippians 4:6, 7, 19 "Be anxious for nothing, but in everything by prayer...with thanksgiving, let your requests be made known to God; and the peace of God, which surpasses all understanding, will guard your hearts and minds through Christ Jesus. And my God shall supply all your need according to His riches in glory by Christ Jesus."

Exodus 15:26 "For I *am* the LORD who heals you."

Isaiah 53:5 "The chastisement for our peace *was* upon Him, And by His stripes we are healed."

Jeremiah 33:3 "Call to Me, and I will answer you, and show you great and mighty things, which you do not know."

Romans 8:28 "And we know that **all things work together for good** to those who love God."

1 John 5:3 "For this is the love of God, that we keep His commandments. And His commandments are not burdensome."[39]

1 John 3:22 "And whatever we ask we receive from Him, because we keep His commandments and do those things that are pleasing in His sight."

Revelation 22:12–14 "I am coming quickly, and My reward *is* with Me, to give every one according to his work. I am the Alpha and the Omega, *the* Beginning and *the* End, the First and the Last. Blessed *are* those who do His commandments, that they may have the right to the tree of life, and may enter through the gates into the city."

Righteous Father, prepare us for this great event, the blessed hope, and the glorious return of our LORD and Savior Jesus Christ, that we can enter through the gates of our real homeland, the New Jerusalem.

Psalm 126:6 "He who continually goes forth weeping, Bearing seed for sowing, Shall doubtless come again with rejoicing, Bringing his sheaves *with him.*"

My hope is to see in heaven all the people on my list, Your answer to my tears and prayers, and to be forever and ever with my LORD, the Lamb of GOD.

There shall be no more death, nor sorrow, nor crying, nor pain.[40] *We returned back to You, we are citizens of heaven, we belong to Your family. We belong to Christ, the King of Kings and LORD of Lords. Everlasting GOD Himself will be with us forever.*

"They shall see His face, and His name shall be on their foreheads" (Revelation 22:4).

---

[39]See "Law/Commandments" in the Topical Bible Reference Index.
[40]See Revelation 21:4.

Praying Step 12

The Work of the Holy Spirit

John 14:16, 17 "And I will pray to the Father, and He will give you another Helper, that He may abide with you forever—the Spirit of truth...for He dwells with you and will be in you."

John 16:13 "He will guide you into all truth; for He will not speak on His own *authority*, but whatever He hears He will speak; and He will tell you things to come."

John 14:26 "But the Helper, the Holy Spirit, whom the Father will send in My name, He will teach you all things, and bring to your remembrance all things that I said to you."

Isaiah 11:2 "The Spirit of the LORD shall rest upon Him, The Spirit of wisdom and understanding, The Spirit of counsel and might, The Spirit of knowledge and of the fear of the LORD."

Jude 1:20, 21 "But you, beloved, building yourselves up on your most holy faith, praying in the Holy Spirit, keep yourselves in the love of God, looking for the mercy of our Lord Jesus Christ unto eternal life."

To empower us to finish Your work, the Spirit blesses us with Your spiritual gifts to support different types of ministry and diverse activities; each one given for the profit of all, enabling us to reach dear souls all around the world. [41]

Loving Father, please help me to understand my part in Your plan—how You would love to use me and the gifts You have given me for Your honor and glory. Your coming is soon, and the work is so great. Many times I am weak and I don't know what to pray for, but I know that my helper, Your Holy Spirit in me, speaks my heart when I can't. [42]

Romans 8:26, 27 "Likewise, the Spirit also helps us in our weaknesses. For we do not know what we should pray for as we ought, but the Spirit Himself makes intercession for us with groanings which cannot be uttered. Now, He [God] who searches the hearts knows what the mind of the Spirit *is*, because He makes intercession for the saints according to *the will of* God."

Heavenly Father, I am so grateful for Your Spirit. Thank You, precious Comforter, for Your work; for You know my deepest and most secret needs. You transform my prayers into the beautiful language of heaven, pleading for me and for each person mentioned,

You transform my prayers into the beautiful language of heaven

---

[41]See Romans 12:4–8; Ephesians 4:11, 12; 1 Corinthians 12:1–11.
[42]See Romans 8:26, 27.

according to the Father's will in order to glorify Him in Heaven. I know My Father will answer in His perfect time and in the best way.

"Now to Him who is able to do exceedingly abundantly above all that we ask or think, according to the power that works in us, to Him be glory…by Christ Jesus to all generations, forever and ever. Amen" (Ephesians 3:20, 21).

May Your name be glorified and Your will be done! Amen.

Benediction: The Word of Our GOD Stands Forever

Everlasting GOD, Your Word and Your promises carry eternal power. It is our heavenly bread, the daily blueprint for our lives. You are eternal. Your Word is eternal. What you say stands forever. It cannot be changed because **You are changeless**. *You ask us to believe the promises in Your Word, to trust; and I do, because You said:*

John 1:1 "In the beginning was the Word, and the Word was with God, and the Word was God."

Hebrews 11:3 "By faith we understand that the worlds were framed by the word of God."

1 John 5:7 "For there are three that bear witness in heaven: the Father, the Word, and the Holy Spirit; and these three are one."

John 1:14 "The Word became flesh and dwelt among us."

Revelation 19:13 "His name is called The Word of God."

Proverbs 30:5 "Every word of God *is* pure; He *is* a shield to those who put their trust in Him."

Titus 1:2 "God, who cannot lie."

John 17:17 "Your word is truth."

Psalm 119:89 "Forever, O Lᴏʀᴅ, Your word is settled in heaven."

Isaiah 40:8 "But the word of our God stands forever."

Jeremiah 23:29 "'*Is* not my word like a fire?' says the Lᴏʀᴅ, 'And like a hammer that breaks the rock in pieces?'"

Hebrews 4:12 "For the word of God is living and powerful, and sharper than any two-edged sword, piercing even to the division of soul and spirit, and of joints and marrow, and is a discerner of the thoughts and intents of the heart."

Isaiah 46:11 "I have spoken *it*; I will also bring it to pass. I have purposed *it*; I will also do it."

Psalm 89:34 "My covenant I will not break, nor alter the word that has gone out of My lips."

Jeremiah 1:12 "For I am ready to perform My word."

Isaiah 55:11 "So shall My word be that goes forth from My mouth; It shall not return to Me void, But it shall accomplish what I please, And it shall prosper *in the thing* for which I sent it."

John 6:63 "The words that I speak to you are spirit, and *they* are life."

Matthew 24:35 "Heaven and earth will pass away, but My words will by no means pass away."

1 Peter 1:23 "The word of God which lives and abides forever."

Because...

Hebrews 13:8 "Jesus Christ *is* the same yesterday, today, and forever."

John 14:6 "I am the way, the truth, and the life. No one comes to the Father except through Me."

Revelation 1:8 "'I am the Alpha and the Omega, *the* Beginning and *the* End,' says the Lord, 'who is and who was and who is to come, the Almighty.'"

"The LORD bless you and keep you; the LORD make His face to shine upon you, and be gracious to you; the LORD lift up His countenance upon you, and give you peace" (Numbers 6:24–26).

Jesus Christ, My All-In-All, Everything That I Need

My LORD Jesus—

You are my Father (Isaiah 63:16)
who first loved me (1 John 4:19).

You formed me (Psalm 139:13)
and know me by name (Isaiah 43:1).

You understand my thoughts from afar (Psalm 139:2)
and keep me in all my ways (Psalm 91:11).

You are my Savior (Luke 1:47),
so merciful and gracious (Psalm 103:8),
who forgives all my sins (Isaiah 1:8).

You are my Redeemer (Isaiah 59:20),
Deliverer (Romans 11:26),
Righteousness (Jeremiah 23:6; 33:16),
and my Confidence (Proverbs 3:26).

You satisfy my hungry soul (Psalm 107:9)
and are my daily Bread (John 6:32–51).

You give me wisdom (Proverbs 2:6).

You lead and guide me in the way I should go (Isaiah 48:17).

You are my Comfort (Isaiah 51:12),
my Shade and Protector (Psalm 121:5, 6),
my Advocate (1 John 2:1),
my Defender (Psalm 59:16),

Jesus Christ, My All-In-All, Everything That I Need

my Keeper (Psalm 121:5),
and my Daily Strength (Psalm 19:14; 31:2).

You are my Helper (Psalm 21:2)
and my Refuge (Psalm 46:1).

You are my Healer (Exodus 15:26),
the One who carries and delivers me (Psalm 46:4).

You are my Shelter and strong Tower (Psalm 61:3),
my Hope (1 Timothy 1:1),
my Peace (Ephesians 2:14),
my Joy (Psalm 5:11),
my Song (Psalm 114:14),
and my Salvation (Psalm 118:14, 21).

You are my Resting Place (Jeremiah 50:6).

You are my Dwelling Place (Psalm 90:1).

You give me life eternal (1 John 5:11)
and wrote my name in Your Book of Life (Revelation 3:5).

You are All That I Need (Colossians 3:11),
my truest Friend (John.15:15).

You love me (Jeremiah 31:3),
You died for me (Colossians 1:20),
and You are coming to take me home (John 14:2, 3),
where I will live with You forever! (John 14:3).

My Savior, my LORD, my GOD—CHRIST JESUS!

The Love of GOD

1 Corinthians 13:1–8 "Though I speak with the tongues of men and of angels, but have not love, I have become sounding brass or a clanging cymbal. And though I have *the gift of* prophecy, and understand all mysteries and all knowledge, and though I have all faith, so that I could remove mountains, but have not love, I am nothing. And though I bestow all my goods to feed *the poor*, and though I give my body to be burned, but have not love, it profits me nothing. Love suffers long *and* is kind; love does not envy; love does not parade itself, is not puffed up; does not behave rudely, does not seek its own, is not provoked, thinks no evil; does not rejoice in iniquity, but rejoices in the truth; bears all things, believes all things, hopes all things, endures all things. **Love never fails**."

1 John 4:7, 8, 11 "**Let us love one another, for love is of God**; and everyone who loves is born of God and knows God. He who does not love does not know God, for **God is love**. Beloved, if God so loved us, we also ought to love one another."

1 John 4:16 "**God is love**, and he who abides in love abides in God, and God in him."

2 Corinthians 13:11 "Be of one mind, live in peace; and the God of love and peace will be with you."

"'And you shall love the LORD your God with all your heart, with all your soul, with all your mind, and with all your strength.' This is the first commandment" (Mark 12:30).

About the Author

The true Author of this booklet is GOD. All glory is due to Him, but He uses His children to bless others. To that end, I was impressed to share these guidelines which have proven effective in my own life.

A little about my background: I grew up in a loving home in Riga, Latvia, one of the old Soviet Republics. My education was as a music educator, piano teacher, and choral conductor which led to many years as a music editor for Latvian TV. It was in 1986, as I was seeking a deeper understanding of GOD's grace, love, and truth, that I feel I finally met my LORD. He changed my life and gave me a passion for spiritual work. I took as my motto the hymn, "Take My Life and Let It Be." I found a new energy in my prayer life and experienced many wonderful answers as leader of my local church's prayer ministry team.

I developed a desire to help spread the Gospel throughout the world, and with the help of an American sponsor, my children's choir recorded several CDs of Christian music, which were distributed to Christian radio stations throughout North America. However, prayer ministry was becoming my main passion.

I am grateful for GOD's wonderful servants who helped me along: one born into the Hebrew tribe of Aaron—Izaks Kleimanis—who eventually became an SDA Pastor and who I count as my spiritual dad, as well as Pastors Alfreds Jakobsons, and Viktors Geide. They and their families have been instrumental in my spiritual growth. Also, my first spiritual sister, Vineta Kraulina, taught me how to pray claiming GOD's promises, a habit which has become my daily strength.

For years I prayed the Prayer of Jabez from 1 Chronicles 4, that GOD "would bless me indeed, and enlarge my territory." He answered by introducing me to my dear husband and partner, Josef, a Canadian, and moving me from the small country of Latvia to Canada, the second largest country in the world. We became a ministry team, reaching souls with GOD's Word, music, instruction in healthy living, and, of course, prayer.

We find prayer to be like oxygen to our souls and studying the Scriptures together to be our spiritual food. Our prayer time starts with reading the Bible together to energize our spirits so that we can pray in accordance with GOD's will as shown in His Word. This booklet was born from that activity.

Currently, we are involved with the prayer ministry group at our church in Ontario. And while all the other ways to reach people for Jesus are important, we have chosen to focus on prayer because no matter your age, income, health status, race, gender, or any other circumstance, everyone can pray. And with the Holy Spirit's power inhabiting the prayers of GOD's people, that is one unstoppable way to reach the millions of people who need to know Jesus and His love.

GOD bless you in your work for Him.

Prayerfully, Anita Sebastian, Ontario, Canada

"There are those all around you who have woes, who need words of sympathy, love, and tenderness, and our humble, pitying prayers."
Ellen G. White[43]

The LORD bless you and keep you,

The LORD make His face shine upon you,

And be gracious to you;

The LORD lift up His countenance upon you,

And give you peace.

Numbers 6:24–26

---

[43]Ellen G. White, *Welfare Ministry* (Washington, DC: Review and Herald Publishing Association, 1952), p. 87.

Topical Bible Reference Index

Heavenly vocabulary to learn or remember, as you read and live.

LORD/Lord: Some translations use all caps in the O.T. then regular case in the N.T. (unless quoting O.T. verses) for GOD the Father and GOD the Son. Psalm 110:1; Matthew 12:8

Truth: 1 John 2:3–5, 21; 3:18; 5:6; John 1:14, 17; 8:31, 32, 45–47; 14:6; 17:17; Ephesians 4:21; Psalm 33:4; 119:142, 151; 3 John 1:2–4, 8

Sin: 1 John 1:7–10; 2:1, 2; 3:4, 6, 8; 5:16–19; Psalm 50:16–18; James 4:17; Revelation 1:5; Isaiah 59:2; Romans 5:12; 7:19–20; Galatians 5:19–21

Death and Resurrection: Romans 6:23; 1 Timothy 6:15, 16; Ecclesiastes 9:5, 6; Psalm 146:3, 4; John 11:11–14; Job 14:10–13; Psalm 115:17; 1 Corinthians 15:51–54; 1 Thessalonians 4:13–17; John 5:28, 29; Daniel 2:2; Matthew 27:52; John 5:28, 29; Revelation 20:1–10

Law/Commandments: 1 John 2:3, 4; 3:4, 5:2–4; Romans 7:7, 12; Psalm 19:7, 8; 119:17, 142; Ecclesiastes 12:13; Romans 7:12; Galatians 3:24; Matthew 5:17, 18; John 13:34, 14:15, 21; 15:10; Psalm 119; Mark 7:6–9; Revelation 11:19; 14:12; 22:14

Satan/Devil: Ezekiel 28:14–17; Isaiah 14:13, 14; Revelation 2:10, 13; 3:9; 20:1–3, 7–10; 12:7–9; John 8:44; 2 Corinthians 11:14; 2 Thessalonians 2:3, 4; Ephesians 6:10–12; 1 Timothy 3:6, 7; 1 Peter 5:8, 9; 1 John 3:8–10

Judge/Judgment: Jeremiah 9:24; Psalm 9:7, 8; 50:4–6; 96:13; 98:9; Matthew 12:36; 16:27; 2 Timothy 4:1; 1 Peter 4:17; 2 Peter 3:7; Jude 1:6, 7; Revelation 15:4; 19:2, 11; 20:4, 11–15

Sanctuary: 1 Kings 8:49; Psalm 2:4; 18:6; 63:2; 96:6; 102:19; 103:19; Hebrews 8:2; 9:6, 8, 12, 24; 33:13–14; Revelation 4:2–11; 8:3–5; 11:19

High Priest: Hebrews 4:14–16; 5; 7; 8; 9:11–28; 10:19–22

New Jerusalem: Isaiah 62:4, 12; 65:17–25; 66:22; Hebrews 11:16; 12:22; Revelation 3:12; 21; 22:1–5

"I will come again"/Christ's return: John 14:1–4; Mark 13; Luke 21:27; Hebrews 7:22–27; Matthew 16:27; 24:27, 30, 31, 36, 37, 42; Acts 1:7, 11; Isaiah 65:17–19; Psalm 50:3; 1 Thessalonians 4:16, 17; 2 Thessalonians 1:7, 9, 10; Jude 1:14; Titus 2:13; 2 Peter 3:11, 12; Revelation 1:7; 3:10–13; 22:12–17

***

The Great Controversy: The ongoing battle between good and evil, which originated in Heaven, between Christ and Satan. We, as humans, are in the middle of this spiritual war. Our Savior longs to restore us; the devil longs to destroy us. Our decisions choose our leader and determine our destiny.

TEACH Services, Inc.
P U B L I S H I N G

We invite you to view the complete
selection of titles we publish at:
www.TEACHServices.com

We encourage you to write us
with your thoughts about this,
or any other book we publish at:
info@TEACHServices.com

TEACH Services' titles may be purchased in
bulk quantities for educational, fund-raising,
business, or promotional use.
bulksales@TEACHServices.com

Finally, if you are interested in seeing
your own book in print, please contact us at:
publishing@TEACHServices.com
We are happy to review your manuscript at no charge.

CPSIA information can be obtained
at www.ICGtesting.com
Printed in the USA
BVHW090748241021
619610BV00003B/69